To:

_____

From:

_____

Date:

_____

a Woman's garden of Love

a Woman's garden of Love

The quoted ideas expressed in this book (but not Scripture verses) are not, in all cases, exact quotations, as some have been edited for clarity and brevity. In all cases, the author has attempted to maintain the speaker's original intent. In some cases, quoted material for this book was obtained from secondary sources, primarily print media. While every effort was made to ensure the accuracy of these sources, the accuracy cannot be guaranteed. For additions, deletions, corrections, or clarifications in future editions of this text, please write Freeman-Smith, LLC.

Scripture taken from the HOLY BIBLE, NEW INTERNATIONAL VERSION ©. NIV ©. Copyright © 1973, 1978, 1984, by International Bible Society. Used by permission of Zondervan Publishing House. All rights reserved.

Scripture quotations marked (NLT) are taken from The Holy Bible, New Living Translation, Copyright © 1996. Used by permission of Tyndale House Publishers, Incorporated, Wheaton, Illinois 60189. All rights reserved.

Scripture quotations are taken from the Holman Christian Standard Bible™, Copyright © 1999, 2000, 2001 by Holman Bible Publishers, used by permission.

Scripture quotations marked (NKJV) are taken from The Holy Bible, New King James Version, Copyright © 1982 by Thomas Nelson, Inc. Used by permission.

Scripture taken from The Message. Copyright © by Eugene H. Peterson 1993, 1994, 1995. Used by permission of NavPress Publishing Group.

Scripture taken from the New American Standard Bible®, Copyright © 1960, 1962, 1963, 1968, 1971, 1972, 1973, 1975, 1977, 1995 by The Lockman Foundation. Used by permission.

Cover Design & Page Layout: Bart Dawson

ISBN 978-1-58334-201-5

Printed in the United States of America

1 2 3 4 5—CHG—16 15 14 13 12

From The Garden
To Your Heart

Table of Contents

The dictionary defines the word *garden* as "a plot of ground used for the cultivation of flowers, fruits, or vegetables." But those of us who regularly dig our hands into the soil know that a garden is *so much more* than a place for growing plants. It is also a place to renew our spirits as we commune with God and marvel at the beauty of His creation.

A garden can be an oasis of sanity amid the pressures and demands of modern-day living. But many of us lack the opportunity or the time to experience the simple joys of sinking our spades into God's good earth. This little book, while no substitute for the garden, is intended to provide similar comforts and pleasures.

In the garden, we gain perspective. In the garden, we renew our strength. In the garden, we spend quiet moments preparing for the harvest *and* preparing for life. And if we are wise, we also offer thanksgiving and praise to the One who has created us and saved us.

Are you the proud keeper of a tidy little garden? If so, give thanks to God every time you go there. But even if you have no garden to plant, or if your field is currently fallow, take time to consider the words on these pages. And remember that the most important seed you'll ever plant is the seed of God's love—through Christ—that you plant forever in your heart.

A Woman's Garden of Love

But now abide faith, hope, love, these three;
but the greatest of these is love.
1 Corinthians 13:13 NASB

Love, like tender young plants in a garden, must be cultivated with care. If we attend to our relationships with a spirit of genuine concern and self-sacrifice, we are blessed. But if we neglect our relationships—or if we seek to manipulate others for our own selfish interests—we reap a bitter harvest indeed.

Our most important relationship is the bond we form with our Heavenly Father and His only begotten Son. When we love God and place Him first in our lives, we find it easier to treat others with the care and respect they deserve. And when we do, they are blessed, and so are we.

*If we love one another,
God abides in us, and
His love is perfected in us.*

1 John 4:12 NASB

Love is an attribute of God.
To love others is evidence of
a genuine faith.
Kay Arthur

Inasmuch as love grows in you, so beauty
grows. For love is the beauty of the soul.
St. Augustine

Line by line, moment by moment, special
times are etched into our memories in
the permanent ink of everlasting love
in our relationships.
Gloria Gaither

It is when we come to the Lord in
our nothingness, our powerlessness, and
our helplessness that He then enables us
to love in a way which, without Him,
would be absolutely impossible.
Elisabeth Elliot

Only God can give us a selfless love
for others, as the Holy Spirit
changes us from within.
Billy Graham

And the Lord make you to increase
and abound in love one toward another,
and toward all men.
1 Thessalonians 3:12 KJV

*Above all, love each other deeply,
because love covers over
a multitude of sins.*

1 Peter 4:8 NIV

I give you a new commandment:
that you love one another.
Just as I have loved you, you
should also love one another.
By this all people will know
that you are My disciples,
if you have love for one another.

John 13:34-35 HCSB

Only joyous love redeems.
Catherine Marshall

Love is not grabbing or self-centered
or selfish. Real love is being able to
contribute to the happiness of another
person without expecting to get
anything in return.
James Dobson

Love is a steady wish for the loved
person's ultimate good.
C. S. Lewis

Love is the seed of all hope.
It is the enticement to trust,
to risk, to try, and to go on.
Gloria Gaither

Love simply cannot spring up without
that self-surrender to each other. If either
withholds the self, love cannot exist.
E. Stanley Jones

Life minus love equals zero.
George Sweeting

A Prayer from the Garden

Lord, love is Your commandment. Help me always to remember that the gift of love is a precious gift indeed. Let me nurture love and treasure it. And, keep me mindful that the essence of love is not to receive it, but to give it, today and forever.

Amen

God's Love

The LORD is gracious and merciful; Slow to anger
and great in lovingkindness. The LORD is good to all,
And His mercies are over all His works.
Psalm 145:8-9 NASB

God's love for you is deeper and more profound than you can fathom. And now, precisely because you are a wondrous creation treasured by God, a question presents itself: What will you do in response to God's love? Will you ignore it or embrace it? Will you return it or neglect it? The decision, of course, is yours and yours alone.

When you embrace God's love, you are forever changed. When you embrace God's love, you feel differently about yourself, your neighbors, and your world. When you embrace God's love, you share His message and you obey His commandments.

When you accept the Father's grace and share His love, you are blessed here on earth and throughout all eternity. Accept His love today.

Beloved, if God so loved us, we ought also to love one another.

1 John 4:11 KJV

Love is not something God does;
love is something God is.
Beth Moore

Being loved by Him whose opinion
matters most gives us the security to risk
loving, too—even loving ourselves.
Gloria Gaither

Snuggle in God's arms. When you are
hurting, when you feel lonely or left out,
let Him cradle you, comfort you, reassure
you of His all-sufficient power and love.
Kay Arthur

*There is no pit so deep that
God's love is not deeper still.*

Corrie ten Boom

The fact is, God no longer deals with us
in judgment but in mercy. If people got
what they deserved, this old planet would
have ripped apart at the seams centuries
ago. Praise God that because of His
great love "we are not consumed,
for His compassions never fail."
Joni Eareckson Tada

The unfailing love of the LORD never ends!
By his mercies we have been kept from
complete destruction.
Lamentations 3:22 NLT

For the Lord your God has arrived to live among you. He is a mighty savior. He will rejoice over you with great gladness. With his love, he will calm all your fears. He will exult over you by singing a happy song.

Zephaniah 3:17 NLT

He created us because
He delights in us!

Beth Moore

The essence of God's being is love—
He never separates Himself from that.
Kay Arthur

You are my God, and I will give you
thanks; you are my God, and I will exalt
you. Give thanks to the LORD, for
he is good; his love endures forever.
Psalm 118:28-29 NIV

The great love of God is an ocean
without a bottom or a shore.
C. H. Spurgeon

Have mercy on me, O God, according
to your unfailing love; according to
your great compassion blot out
my transgressions. Wash away all
my iniquity and cleanse me from my sin.
Psalm 51:1-2 NIV

The last and greatest lesson that the soul
has to learn is the fact that God, and God
alone, is enough for all its needs. This is
the lesson that all His dealings with us are
meant to teach; and this is the crowning
discovery of our whole Christian life.
God is enough!
Hannah Whitall Smith

*The Lord is full of
compassion and mercy.*

James 5:11 NIV

Behold, behold the wondrous love,
That ever flows from God above
Through Christ His only Son, Who gave
His precious blood our souls to save.
Fanny Crosby

Knowing God's sovereignty and
unconditional love imparts a beauty
to life . . . and to you.
Kay Arthur

The whole being of any Christian is Faith
and Love. Faith brings the man to God;
Love brings him to men.
Martin Luther

*This is my commandment,
That ye love one another,
as I have loved you. Greater
love hath no man than this,
that a man lay down his life
for his friends.*

John 15:12-13 KJV

A Prayer from the Garden

Thank You, Lord, for Your love.
Your love is boundless, infinite,
and eternal. Today, let me pause
and reflect upon Your love for
me, and let me share that love
with all those who cross my
path. And, as an expression
of my love for You, Father,
let me share the saving
message of Your Son with
a world in desperate need
of His peace.

Amen

In the Spirit of Kindness

*If I give everything I own to the poor and even go to
the stake to be burned as a martyr, but I don't love,
I've gotten nowhere. So, no matter what I say, what
I believe, and what I do, I'm bankrupt without love.*
1 Corinthians 13:3 MSG

In the busyness and confusion of daily life, it is easy to lose focus, and it is easy to become frustrated. We are imperfect human beings struggling to manage our lives as best we can, but we often fall short. When we are distracted or disappointed, we may neglect to share a kind word or a kind deed. This oversight hurts others, but it hurts us most of all.

Kindness is God's commandment. Matthew 25:40 warns, ". . . Verily I say unto you, Inasmuch as ye have done it unto one of the least of these my brethren, ye have done it unto me" (KJV). When we extend the hand of friendship to those who need it most, God promises His blessings. When we ignore the needs of others—or mistreat them—we risk God's retribution.

Today, slow yourself down and be alert for those who need your smile, your kind words, or your helping hand. Make kindness a centerpiece of your dealings with others. They will be blessed, and you will be too. When you spread a heaping helping of encouragement and hope to the world, you can't help getting a little bit on yourself.

*So in everything, do to others
what you would have them
do to you, for this sums up
the Law and the Prophets.*

Matthew 7:12 NIV

In everything set them an example
by doing what is good.
Titus 2:7 NIV

Don't worry about what you do not
understand. Worry about what you do
understand in the Bible but do not live by.
Corrie ten Boom

There may be no trumpet sound or loud
applause when we make a right decision,
just a calm sense of resolution and peace.
Gloria Gaither

Our lives, we are told, are but fleeting
at best, Like roses they fade and decay;
Then let us do good while the present
is ours, Be useful as long as we stay.
Fanny Crosby

Make it a rule, and pray to God to help
you to keep it, never, if possible, to lie
down at night without being able to say:
"I have made one human being at least
a little wise, or a little happier
or at least a little better this day."
Charles Kingsley

And be kind and compassionate to one
another, forgiving one another,
just as God also forgave you in Christ.
Ephesians 4:32 HCSB

Love one another deeply, from the heart.
1 Peter 1:22 NIV

Let love and faithfulness never
leave you . . . write them
on the tablet of your heart.
Proverbs 3:3 NIV

*Though I speak with the tongues
of men and of angels,
and have not charity,
I am become as sounding brass,
or a tinkling cymbal.*

1 Corinthians 13:1 KJV

A Prayer from the Garden

Lord, make me a woman who clearly sees the needs of those around me. Today, let me show mercy to those who cross my path. Today, let me spread kind words of thanksgiving and celebration in honor of Your Son. Today, let forgiveness rule my heart. And every day, Lord, let my love for Christ be reflected through deeds of kindness for those who need the healing touch of the Master's hand.

Amen

The Gift of

Encouragement

Admonish the unruly, encourage the fainthearted,
help the weak, be patient with everyone.
1 Thessalonians 5:14 NASB

Plants of every sort respond to nourishment, and so it is with human hearts. When we offer encouragement to our family members and friends, we share a form of nourishment that is vital to their spiritual and emotional health.

In the book of Ephesians, Paul writes, "Do not let any unwholesome talk come out of your mouths, but only what is helpful for building others up according to their needs, that it may benefit those who listen" (4:29 NIV). Paul reminds us that when we choose our words carefully, we can have a powerful impact on those around us.

Whether you realize it or not, many people with whom you come in contact every day are in desperate need of a smile or an encouraging word. The world can be a difficult place, and countless friends and family members may be troubled by the challenges of everyday life. Since you don't always know who needs your help, the best strategy is to encourage as many people as you can. So today, be a world-class source of encouragement to everyone you meet. Never has the need been greater.

*Kind words are like honey—
sweet to the soul and healthy
for the body.*

Proverbs 16:24 NLT

*So then we pursue the things which
make for peace and
the building up of one another.*

Romans 14:19 NASB

Words. Do you fully understand their
power? Can any of us really grasp
the mighty force behind the things we say?
Do we stop and think before we speak,
considering the potency of
the words we utter?
Joni Eareckson Tada

If I am asked how we are to get rid
of discouragements, I can only say,
as I have had to say of so many other
wrong spiritual habits, we must give them
up. It is never worthwhile to argue against
discouragement. There is only one
argument that can meet it, and that
is the argument of God.
Hannah Whitall Smith

*Let's see how inventive we can
be in encouraging love and helping
out, not avoiding worshiping
together as some do but
spurring each other on.*

Hebrews 10:24-25 MSG

A cheerful look brings joy to the heart, and good news gives health to the bones.

Proverbs 15:30 NIV

Reject the road to cynicism.
Catherine Marshall

When problems threaten to engulf us,
we must do what believers have always
done, turn to the Lord for encouragement
and solace. As Psalm 46:1 states,
"God is our refuge and strength,
an ever-present help in trouble."
Shirley Dobson

Finally, all of you should be of one mind, full of sympathy toward each other, loving one another with tender hearts and humble minds.

1 Peter 3:8 NLT

A Prayer from the Garden

Lord, make me mindful of
my words. This world can be
a difficult place, and many of
Your children are discouraged
and afraid. Make me a powerful
source of encouragement to
those in need, and let my words
and deeds be worthy of Your
Son, the One who gives me
courage and strength,
this day and for all eternity.

Amen

A Cheerful
Giver

God loves a cheerful giver.
2 Corinthians 9:7 NIV

Hymn writer Fanny Crosby wrote, "To God be the glory; great things He hath done! So loved He the world that He gave us His Son." God's love for us is so complete that He sent Jesus to this earth so that we, His believers, might have eternal life: "But God demonstrates his own love for us in this: While we were still sinners, Christ died for us" (Romans 5:8 NIV).

We, as Christ's followers, are challenged to share His love. We do so, in part, by dealing generously and lovingly with others.

When we walk each day with Christ—and obey the commandments found in God's Holy Word—we are worthy ambassadors for Him. Just as Christ is the ultimate shepherd to His flock, so should we care for those whom God has seen fit to place along our paths. When we give of ourselves and our possessions—and when we do so cheerfully and humbly—we share a priceless gift: the love of Christ. May we share it today and every day that we live.

*Carry each other's burdens,
and in this way you will fulfill
the law of Christ.*

Galatians 6:2 NIV

What is your focus today?
Joy comes when it is Jesus first,
others second . . . then you.
Kay Arthur

And let us not be weary in well doing:
for in due season we shall reap,
if we faint not.
Galatians 6:9 KJV

The Lord has abundantly blessed me all
of my life. I'm not trying to pay Him back
for all of His wonderful gifts; I just realize
that He gave them to me to give away.
Lisa Whelchel

It is when we give ourselves to be
a blessing that we can specially count on
the blessing of God. It is when we draw
near to God as the friend of the poor
and the perishing that we may count
on His friendliness.
Andrew Murray

It is the duty of every Christian
to be Christ to his neighbor.
Martin Luther

A Prayer from the Garden

Lord, You have been so
generous with me; let me be
generous with others. Help me
to give generously of my time
and my possessions as I care
for those in need. And, make
me a humble giver, Lord, so
that all the glory and
the praise might be Yours.

Amen

The Gift
of Laughter

The cheerful heart has a continual feast.
Proverbs 15:15 NIV

Laughter is a gift that we can and should share with our families and friends; it is medicine for the soul, but sometimes, amid the stresses of the day, we forget to take our medicine. Instead of viewing our world with a mixture of optimism and humor, we allow worries and distractions to rob us of the joy that God intends for our lives.

As you go about your daily activities, approach life with a smile on your lips and hope in your heart. And laugh every chance you get. After all, God created laughter for a reason . . . and Father indeed knows best. So laugh!

A keen sense of humor helps us
to overlook the unbecoming,
understand the unconventional, tolerate
the unpleasant, overcome the unexpected,
and outlast the unbearable.
Billy Graham

A happy heart makes
the face cheerful . . . .
Proverbs 15:13 NIV

There is a time for everything,
and a season for every activity under
heaven . . . a time to weep and a time
to laugh, a time to mourn and
a time to dance . . . .
Ecclesiastes 3:1,4 NIV

It is often just as sacred to laugh
as it is to pray.
Charles Swindoll

If our hearts have been attuned to God
through an abiding faith in Christ,
the result will be joyous optimism
and good cheer.
Billy Graham

God is good, and heaven is forever.
And if those two facts can't cheer you up,
nothing can.
Marie T. Freeman

Be cheerful no matter what;
pray all the time; thank God
no matter what happens. This is
the way God wants you who
belong to Christ Jesus to live.

1 Thessalonians 5:16-18 MSG

A Prayer from the Garden

Lord, make me a joyous
Christian. Lord, when I begin
to take myself or my life too
seriously, let me laugh. When I
rush from place to place, slow
me down, Lord, and let me
laugh. Put a smile on my face,
Dear Lord, and let me share
that smile with all who cross
my path . . . and let me laugh.

Amen

The Family Circle

Choose for yourselves this day whom you will serve . . .
as for me and my household, we will serve the LORD.
Joshua 24:15 NIV

A loving family is a treasure from God; if you are a member of a close-knit, supportive family, offer a word of thanks to Him. He has blessed you with one of His most precious earthly possessions.

How should you treat your family? You should care for it, nurture it, and dedicate it to your Creator. When you place God squarely in the center of your family's life—when you worship Him, praise Him, trust Him, and love Him—then God will bless you and yours in ways that you could have scarcely imagined.

He blesses the home of the righteous.

Love

Proverbs 3:33 NIV

We should live so that everybody knows
we're Christians, and most of all,
our families ought to know.
D. L. Moody

A home is a place where we find direction.
Gigi Graham Tchividjian

It is a reverent thing to see an ancient
castle or building not in decay, or to see
a fair timber tree sound and perfect. How
much more beautiful it is to behold an
ancient and noble family that has stood
against the waves and weathers of time.
Francis Bacon

I don't buy the cliché that quality time
with one's family is the most important
thing. If you don't have enough quantity,
you won't get quality.
Leighton Ford

Apart from religious influence, the family
is the most important influence on society.
Billy Graham

The Golden Rule begins at home.
Marie T. Freeman

These should learn first of all to put their religion into practice by caring for their own family.

1 Timothy 5:4 NIV

There is so much compassion and understanding that is gained when we've experienced God's grace firsthand within our own families.

Lisa Whelchel

A Prayer from the Garden

Dear Lord, I am part
of Your family, and I praise You
for Your gifts and Your love.
Father, You have also blessed
me with my earthly family. Let
me show love and acceptance
for my own family so that
through me they might
come to know You.

Amen

The Gift of Friendship

A friend loves at all times.
Proverbs 17:17 NIV

Loyal Christian friendship is ordained by God. Throughout the Bible, we are reminded to love one another, to care for one another, and to treat one another as we wish to be treated. As you journey through the day ahead, please remember the important role that Christian friendship plays in God's plans for His kingdom and for your life.

As Christians, we are commanded to love one another. Today and every day, resolve to be a trustworthy, encouraging, loyal friend. And, treasure those people who are loyal friends to you. Friendship is, after all, a glorious gift, praised by God. Give thanks for that gift and nurture it.

*Love is patient, love is kind and
is not jealous; love does not brag
and is not arrogant, does not act
unbecomingly; it does not seek its
own, is not provoked, does not take
into account a wrong suffered,
does not rejoice in unrighteousness,
but rejoices with the truth; bears
all things, believes all things, hopes
all things, endures all things.*

1 Corinthians 13:4-7 NASB

In friendship, God opens your eyes
to the glories of Himself.
Joni Eareckson Tada

The best times in life are made
a thousand times better when shared
with a dear friend.
Luci Swindoll

If Jesus is the preeminent One in our lives,
then we will love each other, submit to
each other, and treat one another
fairly in the Lord.
Warren Wiersbe

And this commandment have we from him, That he who loveth God love his brother also.

1 John 4:21 KJV

We long to find someone who has been
where we've been, who shares our fragile
skies, who sees our sunsets with
the same shades of blue.
Beth Moore

Brotherly love is still
the distinguishing badge of every
true Christian.
Matthew Henry

Love does no wrong to anyone,
so love satisfies all of God's requirements.
Romans 13:10 NLT

As the Father hath loved me,
so have I loved you;
continue ye in my love.

John 15:9 KJV

A Prayer from the Garden

Lord, You seek abundance
and joy for me and for all Your
children. One way that I can
share Your joy is through the
gift of friendship. Help me to
be a loyal friend. Let me
be ready to listen, ready to
encourage, and ready to offer
a helping hand. Keep me
mindful that I am a servant
of Your Son Jesus. Let me be
a worthy servant, Lord, and
a worthy friend. And, may
the love of Jesus shine through
me today and forever.

Amen

The Gift
of Courtesy

*But the wisdom that comes from heaven is first
of all pure; then peace-loving, considerate, submissive,
full of mercy and good fruit, impartial and sincere.*
James 3:17 NIV

Did Christ instruct us in matters of etiquette and courtesy? Of course He did. Christ's instructions are clear: "In everything, therefore, treat people the same way you want them to treat you, for this is the Law and the Prophets" (Matthew 7:12 NASB). Jesus did not say, "In some things, treat people as you wish to be treated." And, He did not say, "From time to time, treat others with kindness." Christ said that we should treat others as we wish to be treated *in every aspect* of our daily lives. This, of course, is a tall order indeed, but as Christians, we are commanded to do our best.

Today, be a little kinder than necessary to family members, friends, and total strangers. And, as you consider all the things that Christ has done in your life, honor Him with your words and with your deeds. He expects no less, and He deserves no less.

Some people make cutting remarks, but the words of the wise bring healing.

Proverbs 12:18 NLT

Courtesy is contagious.
Marie T. Freeman

When you extend hospitality to others,
you're not trying to impress people;
you're trying to reflect God to them.
Max Lucado

If we have the true love of God in
our hearts, we will show it in our lives.
We will not have to go up and down
the earth proclaiming it. We will show
it in everything we say or do.
D. L. Moody

If my heart is right with God,
every human being is my neighbor.
Oswald Chambers

A soft answer turneth away wrath:
but grievous words stir up anger.
Proverbs 15:1 KJV

*A good person produces good
deeds from a good heart, and
an evil person produces evil deeds
from an evil heart. Whatever is in
your heart determines
what you say.*

Luke 6:45 NLT

Do everything without grumbling
and arguing, so that you may be
blameless and pure.
Philippians 2:14-15 HCSB

Every man's way is right in his own eyes,
but the LORD weighs the hearts.
Proverbs 21:2 NASB

Blessed are the pure in heart:
for they shall see God.
Matthew 5:8 KJV

My dear brothers and sisters, be quick
to listen, slow to speak, and slow to get
angry. Your anger can never make
things right in God's sight.
James 1:19-20 NLT

He who loves to quarrel loves sin . . . .
Proverbs 17:19 NIV

But avoid foolish controversies and geneal-
ogies and arguments and quarrels about
the law, because these are
unprofitable and useless.
Titus 3:9 NIV

But I tell you that anyone who is angry
with his brother is subject to judgment.
Matthew 5:22 NIV

If anyone thinks he is religious, without
controlling his tongue but deceiving
his heart, his religion is useless.
James 1:26 HCSB

Let the words of my mouth, and
the meditation of my heart,
be acceptable in thy sight, O Lord,
my strength and my redeemer.
Psalm 19:14 KJV

A Prayer from the Garden

Help me, Lord, to see the needs
of those around me. Today,
let me show courtesy to those
who cross my path. Today, let
me spread kind words in honor
of Your Son. Today, let
forgiveness rule my heart. And
every day, Lord, let my love for
Christ be reflected through the
acts of kindness that I offer to
those who need the healing
touch of the Master's hand.

Amen

With a Servant's Heart

The greatest among you will be your servant.
For whoever exalts himself will be humbled, and
whoever humbles himself will be exalted.
Matthew 23:10-11 NIV

Martha and Mary both loved Jesus, but they showed their love in different ways. Mary sat at the Master's feet, taking in every word. Martha, meanwhile, busied herself with preparations for the meal to come. When Martha asked Jesus if He was concerned about Mary's failure to help, Jesus replied, "Mary has chosen better" (Luke 10:42 NIV). The implication is clear: as believers, we must spend time with Jesus before we spend time for Him. But, once we have placed Christ where He belongs—at the center of our hearts—we must go about the business of serving the One who has saved us.

How can we serve Christ? By sharing His message and by serving those in need. As followers of Jesus, we must make ourselves humble servants to our families, to our neighbors, and to the world. We must help the helpless, love the unloved, protect the vulnerable, and care for the infirm. When we do, our lives will be blessed by the One who sacrificed His life for us.

*Blessed are those servants,
whom the lord when he cometh
shall find watching. . . .*

Luke 12:37 KJV

Your attitude should be the same as that
of Christ Jesus . . . taking the very nature
of a servant.
Philippians 2:5,7 NIV

God's guidance in all matters is even
more important than common sense.
I can declare that the deepest darkness
is outshone by the light of Jesus.
Corrie ten Boom

Therefore, since we receive a kingdom
which cannot be shaken, let us show
gratitude, by which we may offer
to God an acceptable service
with reverence and awe . . . .
Hebrews 12:28 NASB

Oh, the joys of those who are kind to
the poor. The LORD rescues them
in times of trouble.
Psalm 41:1 NLT

Speak up for those who cannot speak
for themselves, for the rights of all
who are destitute.
Proverbs 31:8 NIV

And above all things have fervent charity
among yourselves: for charity shall cover
the multitude of sins.
1 Peter 4:8 KJV

And he sat down, and called the twelve, and saith unto them, If any man desire to be first, the same shall be last of all, and servant of all.

Mark 9:35 KJV

I tell you the truth, whatever you did for one of the least of these brothers of mine, you did for me.

Matthew 25:40 NIV

A Prayer from the Garden

Dear Lord, when Jesus humbled Himself and became a servant, He also became an example for His followers. Today, as I serve others, I do so in the name of Jesus, my Lord and Master. Guide my steps, Father, and let my service be pleasing to You.

Amen

A Time for Forgiveness

Then Peter came to him and asked, "Lord, how often should I forgive someone who sins against me? Seven times?" "No!" Jesus replied, "seventy times seven! Matthew 18:21-22 NLT

It has been said that life is an exercise in forgiveness. How true. Christ understood the importance of forgiveness when He commanded, "Love your enemies and pray for those who persecute you" (Matthew 5:43-44 NIV). But sometimes, forgiveness is difficult indeed.

When we have been injured or embarrassed, we feel the urge to strike back and to hurt the one who has hurt us. Christ instructs us to do otherwise. Believers are taught that forgiveness is God's way and that mercy is an integral part of God's plan for our lives.

If you bear bitterness against anyone, take your bitterness to God and leave it there. If you are angry, pray for God's healing hand to calm your spirit. If you are troubled by some past injustice, read God's word and remember His commandment to forgive. When you follow that commandment and sincerely forgive those who have hurt you, you'll discover that a heavy burden has been lifted from your shoulders. And, you'll discover that, although forgiveness is indeed difficult, with God's help all things are possible.

*Do not let the sun go down
on your anger, and do not give
the devil an opportunity.*

Ephesians 4:26-27 NASB

Forgiveness is the precondition of love.
Catherine Marshall

Forgiveness is not an emotion.
Forgiveness is an act of the will, and
the will can function regardless of
the temperature of the heart.
Corrie ten Boom

I believe that forgiveness can become
a continuing cycle: because God forgives
us, we're to forgive others; because
we forgive others, God forgives us.
Scripture presents both parts of the cycle.
Shirley Dobson

*Forgiveness is the key that
unlocks the door of resentment
and the handcuffs of hate.
It is a power that breaks
the chains of bitterness and
the shackles of selfishness.*

Corrie ten Boom

Do not take revenge, my friends, but leave
room for God's wrath, for it is written:
"It is mine to avenge; I will repay," says
the Lord. On the contrary: "If your enemy
is hungry, feed him; if he is thirsty, give
him something to drink. In doing this,
you will heap burning coals on his head."
Do not be overcome by evil,
but overcome evil with good.
Romans 12:19-21 NIV

All bitterness, anger and wrath, insult
and slander must be removed from you,
along with all wickedness. And be kind
and compassionate to one another,
forgiving one another, just as God
also forgave you in Christ.
Ephesians 4:31-32 HCSB

*Our relationships with other people
are of primary importance
to God. Because God is love,
He cannot tolerate any
unforgiveness or hardness in us
toward any individual.*

Catherine Marshall

*He who cannot forgive others
breaks the bridge over which
he himself must pass.*

Corrie ten Boom

I have set you an example that you should do as I have done for you.

John 13:15 NIV

But love ye your enemies, and do good,
and lend, hoping for nothing again; and
your reward shall be great, and ye shall be
the children of the Highest . . . .
Luke 6:35 KJV

And whenever you stand praying, if you
have anything against anyone, forgive him,
so that your Father in heaven may
also forgive you your wrongdoing.
Mark 11:25 HCSB

*Keep your face upturned
to Christ as the flowers do to the
sun. Look, and your soul
shall live and grow.*

Hannah Whitall Smith

A Prayer from the Garden

Lord, make me a woman who
is slow to anger and quick to
forgive. When I am bitter, You
can change my unforgiving
heart. And, when I am angry,
Your Word reminds me
that forgiveness is Your
commandment. Let me be
Your obedient servant, Lord,
and let me forgive others just
as You have forgiven me.

Amen

Celebrating Others

*A word aptly spoken is like apples of gold
in settings of silver.*
Proverbs 25:11 NIV

Do you delight in the victories of others? You should. Each day provides countless opportunities to encourage others and to praise their good works. When you do so, you not only spread seeds of joy and happiness, you also obey the commandments of God's Holy Word.

Life is a team sport, and all of us need occasional pats on the back from our teammates. As Christians, we are called upon to spread the Good News of Christ, and we are also called to spread a message of encouragement and hope to the world.

Today, let us be cheerful Christians with smiles on our faces and encouraging words on our lips. By blessing others, we also bless ourselves, and, at the same time, we do honor to the One who gave His life for us.

*So then, let us aim for harmony
in the church and try
to build each other up.*

Romans 14:19 NLT

Be united with other Christians. A wall with loose bricks is not good. The bricks must be cemented together.

Corrie ten Boom

How good and pleasant it is
when brothers live together in unity!
Psalm 133:1 NIV

Christ is with us . . . and the warmth
is contagious.
Joni Eareckson Tada

Kind words are like honey—sweet to
the soul and healthy for the body.
Proverbs 16:24 NLT

A Prayer from the Garden

Dear Lord, let me celebrate
the accomplishments of others.
Make me a source of genuine,
lasting encouragement to my
family and friends. And let my
words and deeds be worthy
of Your Son, the One who gives
me strength and salvation,
this day and for all eternity.

Amen

Love for Our Creator, Love for Our Savior

Jesus replied, "'Love the Lord your God with all your heart and with all your soul and with all your mind.' This is the first and greatest commandment. And the second is like it: 'Love your neighbor as yourself.' All the Law and the Prophets hang on these two commandments."
Matthew 22:37-40 NIV

In the garden, we sense God's presence and His love. And as God's children, we are called to return the Father's love.

Christ made it clear: our first and greatest commandment is that we love God with all our hearts. When we worship God with faith and assurance, when we place Him at the absolute center of our lives, we invite His love into our hearts. When we do so, we are blessed beyond measure and beyond words.

St. Augustine wrote, "I love You, Lord, not doubtingly, but with absolute certainty. Your Word beat upon my heart until I fell in love with You, and now the universe and everything in it tells me to love You." Let us pray that we, too, will turn our hearts to our Father and to His Son. When we do, we are blessed in this life and throughout all eternity.

For I am persuaded,
that neither death, nor life,
nor angels, nor principalities,
nor powers, nor things present,
nor things to come, nor height, nor
depth, nor any other creature, shall
be able to separate us from
the love of God, which is in
Christ Jesus our Lord.

Romans 8:38-39 KJV

But God demonstrates his own love for us in this: While we were still sinners, Christ died for us.

Romans 5:8 NIV

When once we are assured that God is good, then there can be nothing left to fear.
Hannah Whitall Smith

The unfolding of our friendship with the Father will be a never-ending revelation stretching on into eternity.
Catherine Marshall

Our hearts are prone to wander
and tempted to squander our Father's
inheritance on the world's cheap
amusements. But, when our eyes awaken
to reality, when we lift our heads above
the compromise, and when our stomachs
ache for the food of home, a certain
Father will always be standing at the gate,
ready to prepare a feast for us, waiting
anxiously for His prodigal to come home.
Beth Moore

Our souls were made to live in an upper
atmosphere, and we stifle and choke if
we live on any lower level. Our eyes were
made to look off from these heavenly
heights, and our vision is distorted
by any lower gazing.
Hannah Whitall Smith

This is my song through endless ages:
Jesus led me all the way.

Fanny Crosby

Christ is risen! Hallelujah!
Gladness fills the world today;
From the tomb that could not hold Him,
See, the stone is rolled away!
Fanny Crosby

Let us run with endurance the race that
is set before us, fixing our eyes on Jesus,
the author and perfecter of faith.
Hebrews 12:1-2 NASB

Jesus intended for us to be overwhelmed
by the blessings of regular days. He said it
was the reason He had come: "I am come
that they might have life, and that they
might have it more abundantly."
Gloria Gaither

*I came that they may have life,
and have it abundantly.*

John 10:10 NASB

*For the Son of man is come
to save that which was lost.*

Matthew 18:11 KJV

The crucial question for each of us is this: What do you think of Jesus, and do you yet have a personal acquaintance with Him?

Hannah Whitall Smith

I think God knew that the message
we sometimes need to hear today is not
what a great and mighty God we serve,
but rather what a tender,
loving Father we have.
Lisa Whelchel

Until now you have asked for nothing
in My name. Ask and you will receive,
that your joy may be complete.
John 16:24 HCSB

Jesus is all compassion.
He never betrays us.
Catherine Marshall

*Jesus Christ the same yesterday,
and today, and for ever.*

Hebrews 13:8 KJV

Even before God created the heavens
and the earth, He knew you and me,
and He chose us! You and I were born
because it was God's good pleasure.
Kay Arthur

Has He taken over your heart?
Perhaps He resides there, but
does He preside there?
Vance Havner

There is a God-shaped hole in every
man that only God can fill.
St. Augustine

Love is not merely an attitude with which
God clothes Himself at certain times; rather, it is an attribute that so permeates His
being that He could never divest Himself
of it. To do so would make Him less than
God. Therefore, whatever actions or commandments issue forth from
His throne must come from love.

Kay Arthur

Unfailing love surrounds those
who trust the LORD.

Psalm 32:10 NLT

*Love the Lord your God
with all your heart and with
all your soul and with
all your strength.*

Deuteronomy 6:5 NIV

This is how we know that we love
the children of God: by loving God
and carrying out his commands.
1 John 5:2 NIV

Obedience is the outward expression
of your love of God.
Henry Blackaby

There may be no trumpet sound or loud
applause when we make a right decision,
just a calm sense of resolution and peace.
Gloria Gaither

Delighting thyself in the Lord is
the sudden realization that He has
become the desire of your heart.
Beth Moore

Yielding to the will of God is simply letting
His Holy Spirit have His way in our lives.
Shirley Dobson

Telling the Lord how much you love
Him and why is what praise and
worship are all about.
Lisa Whelchel

Yes, God's grace is always
sufficient, and His arms
are always open to give it.
But, will our arms be
open to receive it?

Beth Moore

Oh! what a Savior, gracious to all,
Oh! how His blessings round us fall,
Gently to comfort, kindly to cheer,
Sleeping or waking, God is near.
Fanny Crosby

Everything I possess of any worth
is a direct product of God's love.
Beth Moore

Put your hand into the hand of God.
He gives the calmness and serenity
of heart and soul.
Mrs. Charles E. Cowman

*Those who are God's
without reserve are,
in every sense, content.*

Hannah Whitall Smith

Who is it that is your Shepherd?
The Lord! Oh, my friends, what
a wonderful announcement! The Lord
God of heaven and earth, and Almighty
Creator of all things, He
who holds the universe in His hand as
though it were a very little thing. He is
your Shepherd and has charged Himself
with the care and keeping of you, as a
shepherd is charged with the care and
keeping of his sheep. If your hearts
could really take in this thought,
you would never have a fear or a care
again, for with such a Shepherd
how could it be possible for you ever
to want any good thing?

Hannah Whitall Smith

The LORD is my shepherd; I shall not want. He maketh me to lie down in green pastures: he leadeth me beside the still waters. He restoreth my soul: he leadeth me in the paths of righteousness for his name's sake. Yea, though I walk through the valley of the shadow of death, I will fear no evil: for thou art with me; thy rod and thy staff they comfort me. Thou preparest a table before me in the presence of mine enemies: thou anointest my head with oil; my cup runneth over. Surely goodness and mercy shall follow me all the days of my life: and I will dwell in the house of the LORD for ever.

Psalm 23 KJV

Be strong and of a good courage;
be not afraid, neither be thou dismayed:
for the LORD thy God is with thee
whithersoever thou goest.
Joshua 1:9 KJV

I will lift up mine eyes unto the hills,
from whence cometh my help.
Psalm 121:1 KJV

And God will generously provide all
you need. Then you will always have
everything you need and plenty left over
to share with others.
2 Corinthians 9:8 NLT

Let your gentleness be evident to all. The Lord is near.

Philippians 4:5 NIV

In God's faithfulness lies eternal security.
Corrie ten Boom

I will sing of the LORD'S great love
forever; with my mouth I will make your
faithfulness known through all generations.
Psalm 89:1 NIV

And we know that all things work
together for good to them that love God,
to them who are the called according
to his purpose.
Romans 8:28 KJV

We love him,
because he first loved us.

1 John 4:19 KJV

A Prayer from the Garden

Dear Heavenly Father,
You have blessed me with a love
that is infinite and eternal. Let
me love You, Lord, more and
more each day. Make me a
loving servant, Father, today
and throughout eternity. And,
let me show my love for You
by sharing Your message and
Your love with others.

Amen

And the Greatest of These Is Love

*Love never gives up. Love cares more for others than
for self. Love doesn't want what it doesn't have.
Love doesn't strut, Doesn't have a swelled head, Doesn't
force itself on others, Isn't always "me first," Doesn't fly
off the handle, Doesn't keep score of the sins of others,
Doesn't revel when others grovel, Takes pleasure in
the flowering of truth, Puts up with anything, Trusts
God always, Always looks for the best,
Never looks back, But keeps going to the end.*
1 Corinthians 13:4-7 MSG

Christ's words are unambiguous: "'Love the Lord your God with all your heart and with all your soul and with all your mind.' This is the first and greatest commandment. And the second is like it: 'Love your neighbor as yourself.' All the Law and the Prophets hang on these two commandments" (Matthew 22:37-40 NIV). But sometimes, despite our best intentions, we fail to obey our Lord. When we become embittered with ourselves, with our neighbors, or most especially with God, we disobey the One who gave His life for us.

In 1 Corinthians 13, we are told that love is the foundation upon which all our relationships are to be built: our relationships with others *and* our relationship with our Creator. Today and every day, may we fill our hearts with love; may we never yield to the spiritual poisons of hatred or bitterness. And may we praise the Son of God who, in His infinite wisdom, made love His greatest commandment.

*God is love; and he that dwelleth
in love dwelleth in God,
and God in him.*

1 John 4:16 KJV

But seek ye first the kingdom of God,
and his righteousness; and all these things
shall be added unto you.
Matthew 6:33 KJV

He who pursues righteousness and
love finds life, prosperity and honor.
Proverbs 21:21 NIV

But prove yourselves doers of the word,
and not merely hearers who delude
themselves.
James 1:22 NASB

And what does the Lord require of you? To act justly and to love mercy and to walk humbly with your God.

Micah 6:8 NIV

You are the light of the world. A city on a hill cannot be hidden. Neither do people light a lamp and put it under a bowl. Instead they put it on its stand, and it gives light to everyone in the house. In the same way, let your light shine before men, that they may see your good deeds and praise your Father in heaven.

Matthew 5:14-16 NIV

*And the most important piece
of clothing you must wear is love.
Love is what binds us all together
in perfect harmony.*

Colossians 3:14 NLT

A Prayer from the Garden

Dear God, let me share Your love with the world. Make me a woman of compassion. Help me to recognize the needs of others. Let me forgive those who have hurt me, just as You have forgiven me. And let the love of Your Son shine in me and through me today, tomorrow, and throughout all eternity.

Amen